Pebble™ Plus

A Visit to

The Zoo

by B. A. Hoena

Consulting Editor: Gail Saunders-Smith, Ph.D.
Reading Consultant: Jennifer Norford, Senior Consultant
Mid-continent Research for Education and Learning
Aurora, Colorado

Capstone press

Mankato, Minnesota

Pebble Plus is published by Capstone Press
151 Good Counsel Drive, P.O. Box 669, Mankato, Minnesota 56002
www.capstonepress.com

1 2 3 4 5 6 09 08 07 06 05 04

Library of Congress Cataloging-in-Publication Data
Hoena, B. A.
The zoo/by B. A. Hoena.
p. cm.—(Pebble plus. A visit to)
Includes bibliographical references and index.
Contents: The zoo—Zoo animals—Zookeepers—Around the zoo.
ISBN 0-7368-2395-6 (hardcover)
1. Zoos—Juvenile literature. 2. Zoo animals—Juvenile literature. [1. Zoos. 2. Zoo animals.] I. Title. II. Series.
QL76.H64 2004
636.088'9—dc22   2003011995

Editorial Credits
Sarah L. Schuette, editor; Jennifer Bergstrom, series designer; Kelly Garvin, photo researcher;
   Karen Risch, product planning editor

Photo Credits
Bruce Coleman Inc./Barbara P. Williams, 10–11; Joan Iaconetti, 5; John Elk III, 9; John Giust, 21; Kenneth Fink, 7
David R. Frazier Photolibrary, 13
Index Stock Imagery/Carl Scofield, 19; Jeff Greenberg, 16–17
James P. Rowan, 1, 14–15
PhotoDisc Inc., cover (boy, tree, rock), back cover
Ralf Schmode, cover (tigers)

Note to Parents and Teachers

The series A Visit to supports national social studies standards related to the production,
distribution, and consumption of goods and services. This book describes and illustrates
the zoo. The images support early readers in understanding the text. The repetition of
words and phrases helps early readers learn new words. This book also introduces early
readers to subject-specific vocabulary words, which are defined in the Glossary section.
Early readers may need assistance to read some words and to use the Table of Contents,
Glossary, Read More, Internet Sites, and Index/Word List sections of the book.

Word Count: 125
Early-Intervention Level: 12

Table of Contents

The Zoo

The zoo is a busy place
to visit. People go to the
zoo to see many animals.

Zoo Animals

Lions rest on rocks or under trees. Lions rest during the day.

Jellyfish swim in tanks.

The jellyfish pump water

in and out of their bodies

to move.

Parrots perch on branches.

They have sharp beaks

and strong feet.

Zookeepers

Zookeepers work in zoos.

They take care of foxes

and other zoo animals.

13

Zookeepers feed zoo
animals. They feed fish
to sea lions.

Zookeepers teach visitors about zoo animals. They hold snakes and other animals for visitors to touch.

Around the Zoo

The petting zoo is the home
for some animals. Zoo
visitors can touch and feed
sheep, goats, and horses.

A zoo is a place to

have fun, play, and learn.

Glossary

fox—a wild animal with thick fur, a pointed nose and ears, and a bushy tail

jellyfish—a sea animal with a soft body and tentacles

lion—a large wildcat; male lions have manes.

parrot—a tropical bird with a curved beak and brightly colored feathers

perch—to sit or stand on the edge of something

sea lion—a seal with large flippers and ears that stick out; sea lions are mammals.

Read More

Canizares, Susan. *At the Zoo.* Scholastic Placebook. New York: Scholastic, 2000.

Deady, Kathleen W. *Out and About at the Zoo.* Field Trips. Minneapolis: Picture Window Books, 2003.

Foley, Cate. *Let's Go to the Zoo.* Weekend Fun. New York: Children's Press, 2001.

Internet Sites

FactHound offers a safe, fun way to find Internet sites related to this book. All of the sites on FactHound have been researched by our staff.

Here's how:

1. Visit *www.facthound.com*

2. Type in this special code **0736823956** for age-appropriate sites. Or enter a search word related to this book for a more general search.

3. Click on the **Fetch It** button.

FactHound will fetch the best sites for you!

23

Index/Word List